D1162057

OCTOPUS

JOSH PLATTNER

CONSULTING EDITOR, DIANE CRAIG, M.A./READING SPECIALIST

Super Sandcastle

An Imprint of Abdo Publishing
abdopublishing.com

abdopublishing.com

Published by Abdo Publishing, a division of ABDO, PO Box 398166, Minneapolis, Minnesota 55439.

Printed in the United States of America, North Mankato, Minnesota
062015
092015

Editor: Liz Salzmann
Content Developer: Nancy Tuminelly
Cover and Interior Design and Production: Anders Hanson, Mighty Media, Inc.
Photo Credits: Shutterstock

Library of Congress Cataloging-in-Publication Data
Plattner, Josh, author.
Octopus : master of disguise / Josh Plattner ; consulting editor, Diane Craig, M.A./reading specialist.
pages cm. -- (Animal superpowers)
Audience: K to grade 4
ISBN 978-1-62403-737-5
1. Octopuses--Juvenile literature. I. Title.
QL430.3.O2P53 2016
594.56--dc23
2014048272

Super SandCastle™ books are created by a team of professional educators, reading specialists, and content developers around five essential components—phonemic awareness, phonics, vocabulary, text comprehension, and fluency—to assist young readers as they develop reading skills and strategies and increase their general knowledge. All books are written, reviewed, and leveled for guided reading, early reading intervention, and Accelerated Reader™ programs for use in shared, guided, and independent reading and writing activities to support a balanced approach to literacy instruction.

CONTENTS

AWESOME OCTOPUS 4

CRAZY CAMOUFLAGE 6

AMAZING ARMS 8

MAGIC MOVEMENT 10

SPECTACULAR SENSES 12

DIFFERENT DEFENSES 14

BRUTAL BEAK 16

HOLY HEARTS! 18

SEA SMARTS 20

OCTOPUS SUPERHERO 22

WHAT DO YOU KNOW ABOUT OCTOPUSES? 23

GLOSSARY 24

AWESOME OCTOPUS

There are more than 300 **species** of Octopus. They are all **cephalopods**.

HOW BIG ARE THEY?

They can be 14 feet (4.3 m) long. Big ones weigh around 30 pounds (15 kg). The largest recorded octopus was 157 pounds (71 kg)!

CRAZY CAMOUFLAGE

What is this animal's superpower? **Camouflage**! Octopuses can change color. Their **texture** can also change.

Camouflage hides them from predators. It also warns other octopuses.

AMAZING ARMS

Octopuses have eight arms. They're each covered with **suction cups**. These cups help octopuses grab objects. They also help them catch their next meal.

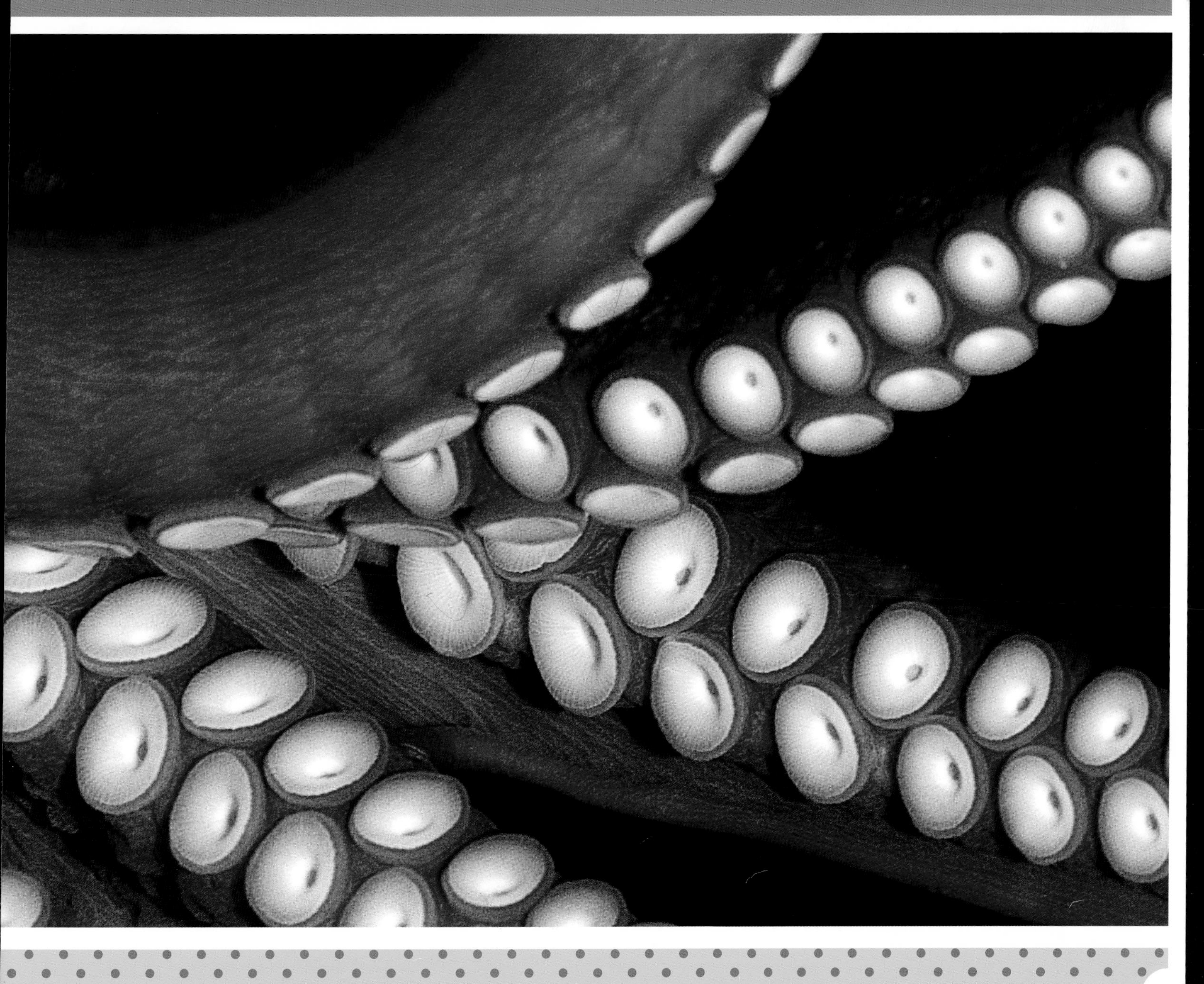

MAGIC MOVEMENT

Octopuses live in the ocean. They swim through the water. They can also crawl on the ocean floor.

JETTING

Octopuses shoot water out of their bodies. This helps them move faster. It is called jetting.

SPECTACULAR SENSES

Octopuses have great eyesight. They can see well underwater.

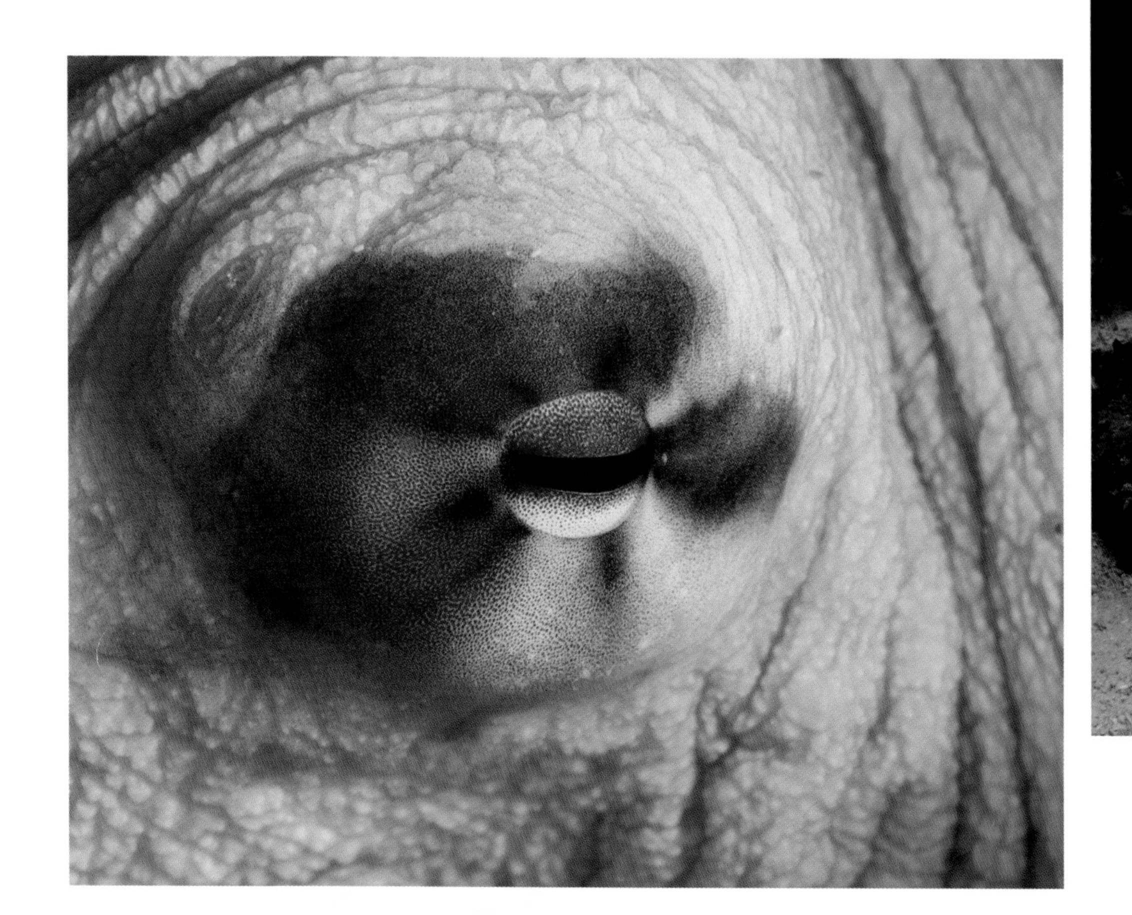

They also have a great sense of touch. They can taste through touching!

DIFFERENT DEFENSES

Camouflage isn't an octopus's only **defense.** It also has ink. It shoots the ink from an ink **sac.**

The ink blinds predators. It also blocks the predators' sense of smell.

BRUTAL BEAK

An octopus has a beak. It's the only hard part of its body.

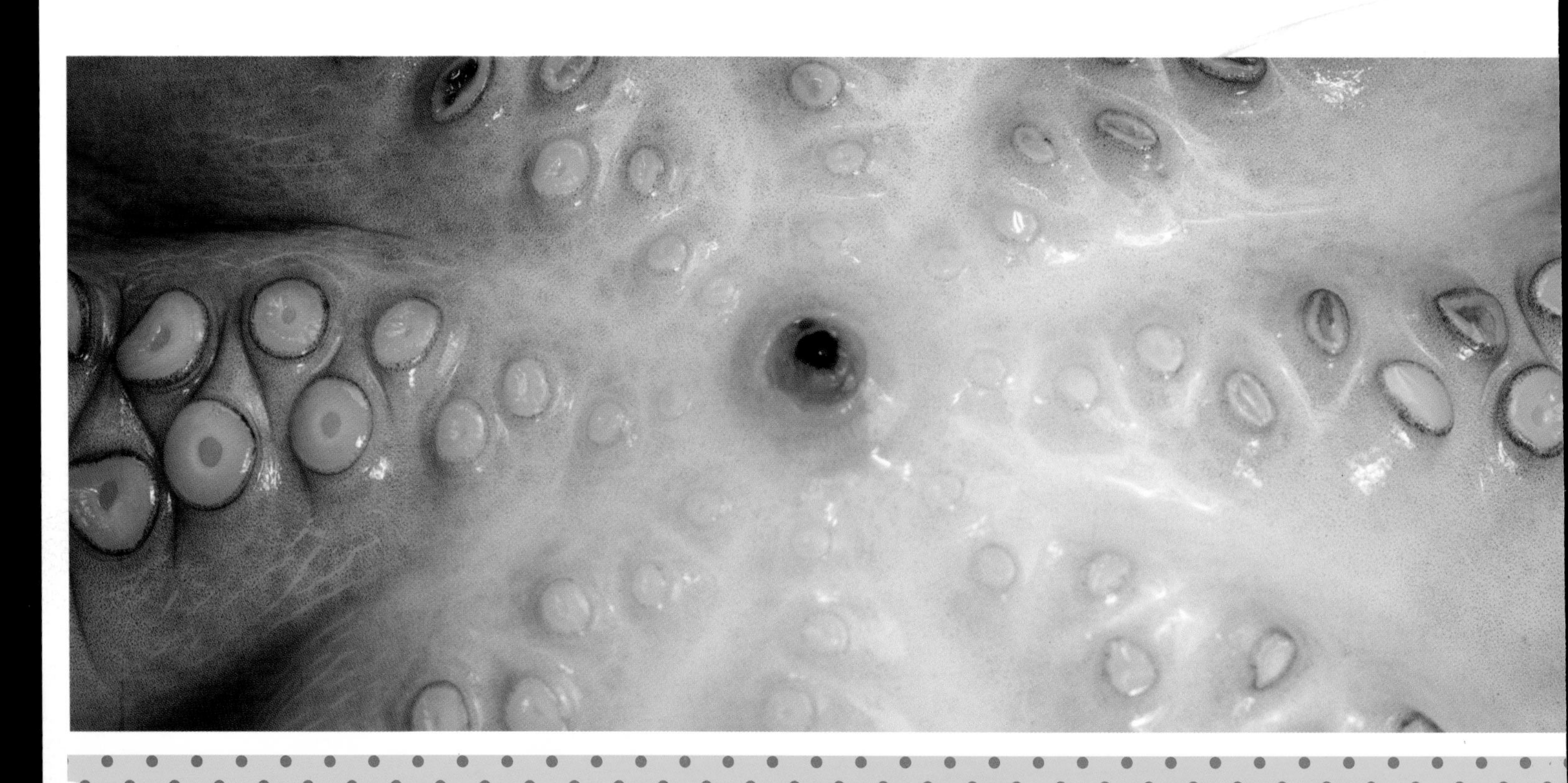

WHAT DOES AN OCTOPUS EAT?

Octopuses use their beaks to break the shells of crabs and clams.

Octopuses also eat small fish.

HOLY HEARTS!

Octopuses have three hearts. Two pump blood to the gills. One is for the left and one is for the right. The third heart pumps blood throughout the rest of the body.

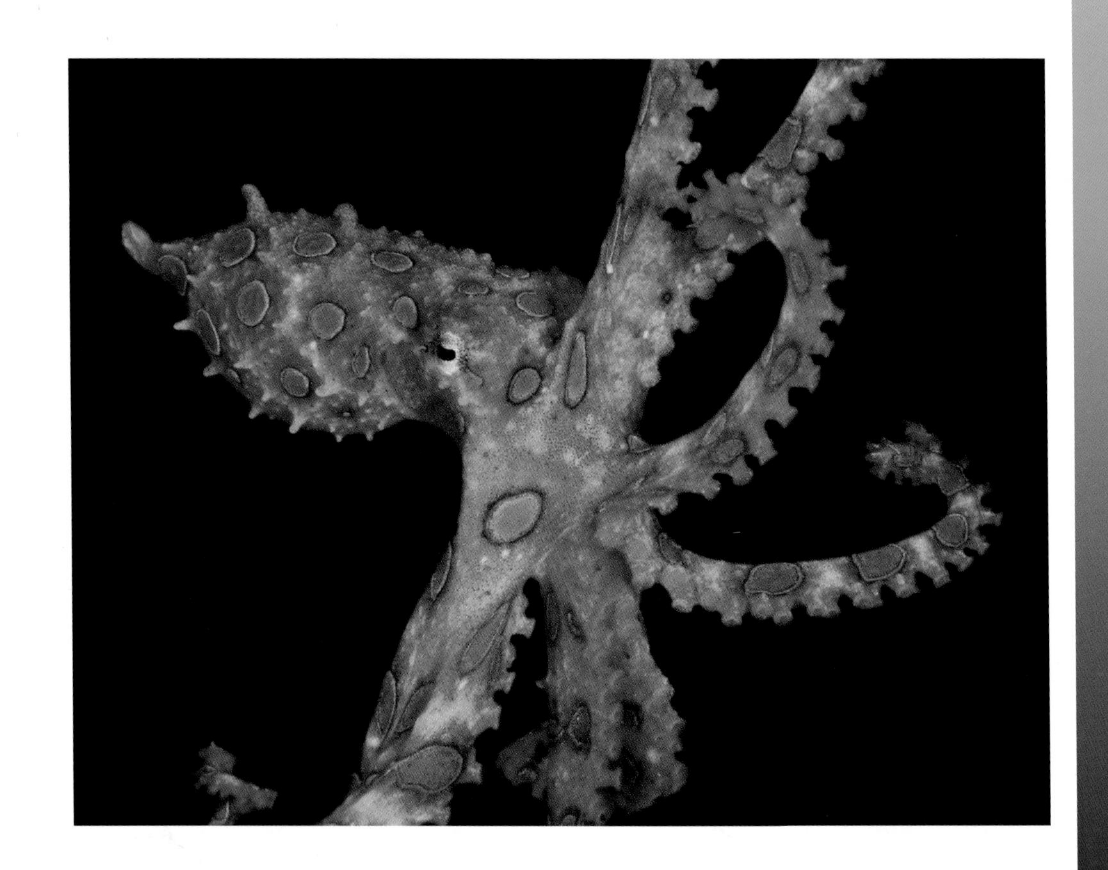

SEA SMARTS

Octopuses are very intelligent. They have great memory skills. They can learn how to use tools.

They recycle **materials** to create shelters.

OCTOPUS SUPERHERO

Can you imagine an octopus superhero? What would it look like? What could it do?

WHAT DO YOU KNOW ABOUT

OCTOPUSES?

1. An octopus's superpower is **camouflage**.

TRUE OR FALSE?

2. Octopuses can see well underwater.

TRUE OR FALSE?

3. Octopuses don't eat small fish.

TRUE OR FALSE?

4. Octopuses have three hearts.

TRUE OR FALSE?

ANSWERS:

1. TRUE 2. TRUE 3. FALSE 4. TRUE

GLOSSARY

CAMOUFLAGE - the features of an animal that make it look like its surroundings.

CEPHALOPOD - the animal class that includes squids, cuttlefishes, and octopuses.

DEFENSE - the act or means of protecting from harm or attack.

MATERIAL - something that other things can be made of, such as fabric, plastic, or metal.

SAC - a pouch that is part of a plant's or animal's body.

SPECIES - a group of related living beings.

SUCTION CUP - a flexible cup that sticks when the open end is pressed to a flat surface.

TEXTURE - what something feels like, such as rough, smooth, hard, or soft.